CORAL REEF ANIMALS FOR KIDS

Habitat Facts, Photos and Fun

Children's Oceanography

Books Edition

Speedy Publishing LLC
40 E. Main St. #1156
Newark, DE 19711
www.speedypublishing.com

The coral reef is one of the
major marine biomes. Coral
reefs are generally found
in clear, tropical oceans.

Clownfish are
small in size.
They can reach
between 2
and 5 inches in
length. Clownfish
is immune to
the venom of
anemone because
it has thick layer
of mucus on
the surface
of the body.

Clownfish are found in warm waters of the Indian and Pacific Oceans including the Red Sea and the Great Barrier Reef of Australia.

Sea anemones look like flowers but they are actually animals. Sea anemones use their tentacles to sting the shrimps, fish, and other small animals that they eat.

Sea anemones are
found throughout
the world's oceans
at various depths,
although the largest
and most varied
occur in coastal
tropical waters.

Lionfish are famous by their beautifully colored bodies, covered with red, white, orange, black or brown stripes. Lionfish has more than thirteen venomous spines on the back side of the body.

Lionfish are found
in the South Pacific
Ocean. They like to
live in coral reefs,
rocky areas,
and lagoons.

A seahorse is a
fish. Seahorses
eat plankton and
small crustaceans.
They do not have
teeth and stomach
and food passes
quickly through
their body.

Seahorses prefer shallow water and they are usually located near coral reefs, mangrove forests or near the seaweed.

The cuttlefish is a mollusk and is closely related to the octopus. Cuttlefish can change color to blend into the background, avoid enemies and grab food more easily.

They are found
in shallow reefs
or channels up
to 80 feet. They
are native to the
Mediterranean and
Eastern Atlantic.

Sea turtles are reptiles. Sea turtles are very old organisms. They live on the Earth more than 220 million years.

Sea turtles can
be found in all
oceans of the
world except in
the polar area.

Giant clam is a
huge mollusk.
Giant clam has
thick, bony shell
that can be easily
recognized by its
zigzag shape.

Giant clam inhabits
coral reefs and
lagoons. It can
be found in the
tropical waters of
Indian and Pacific
oceans, in Thailand,
Japan, Micronesia
and Australia.

Starfish belongs
to a large group
of marine
animals called
echinoderms.
Starfish is a
carnivore who
likes to eat clams,
shells and mussels.

Starfish are
usually located in
the shallow water.
They can be
found in all oceans
of the world.

Sea urchins have spiny shells for protection. Some of the species have poisonous soft spines. Sea urchins are omnivorous animals and therefore eat both plant and animal matter.

Sea urchins are commonly found along the rocky ocean floor in both shallow and deeper water and sea urchins are also commonly found inhabiting coral reefs.